I0475090

Great Hotel Service

101 Ways to Create Great Customer Service and Experience in the Hospitality Industry

Orkun Avkan

New York City Books

Great Hotel Service
101 Ways to Create Great Customer Service and Experience
in the Hospitality Industry
Orkun Avkan

Copyright ©2019 Orkun Avkan

ISBN: 9781077139947

All Rights Reserved
Including the right of reproduction in whole or in part in any
form.

Published by New York City Books
www.nycitybooks.com

Illustrated By Naz Sirmen
Edited By Mehmet Gökdel
Translated By Abdullah Çeçen

Library of Congress Cataloging-in-Publication Data
Avkan, Orkun
101 Ways to Guest Satisfaction
Subjects:
1. Guest Service 2. Customer Service 3. Hospitality
Management

Great Hotel Service

Orkun Avkan

BIOGRAPHY

Orkun Avkan worked as a professional for the esteemed hotel chains such as Ritz Carlton, Four Seasons, and Hilton. During his career for more than 25 years in Europe and the US, he observed and analyzed the pitfalls of the hospitality industry as well as what makes a great service. He designed training programs based on his analysis, observations, experience, and research in the hotel industry. Besides continuing his professional career in the hotel industry, he delivered speeches about guest service beyond expectations and trained the hotel industry staff. He believes in the essence of excellent service is the people, but not ordinary people, trained and customer oriented people. He dedicated his life to improving service quality in the hospitality industry.

As a proven hotelier, Orkun is sharing the key points of guest satisfaction. It is an essential guide for all hoteliers as well as people who works is service industry. The book is full of real experiences; sharp, inspiring and funny. I gave it as a present to all my department heads.
A must have precious book.
Alper Can Bulcum
San Clemente Palace Kempinski Venice
General Manager

Great Hotel Service provides practical tips and principles for the hospitality industry. It's a must read for every team member at a hotel.
Nikolay Tevekeliyski
Chief Experience Officer
The Cosmopolitan Group

"Great Hotel Service is easy to read and understand, but profound in so many ways! If hotel managers and employees would follow this advice, their guests and business would be significantly better."
Mel Arat,
CEO, Author,
Innovation as a Lifestyle

TABLE OF CONTENTS

31 DON'T MAKE PROMISES THAT YOU CAN'T KEEP
32 NEVER SAY NO TO YOUR GUESTS
33 USE MAGICAL EXPRESSIONS: "CERTAINLY, SURE, WITH PLEASURE"
34 DON'T BECOME FRIENDS WITH THE GUESTS
35 RESPECT THE GUESTS' PRIVATE LIFE
36 DON'T TALK ABOUT YOUR PRIVATE LIFE
37 RESPECT INCOGNITO
38 HELP TO CELEBRATE SPECIAL DAYS OF YOUR GUESTS
39 COMMUNICATE EFFECTIVELY
40 CHEAP PRODUCT EXPENSIVE COMPLAINT
41 WATCH OUT FOR OPPORTUNITIES TO DO GOOD THINGS
42 KNOW YOUR GUEST
43 LITTLE COMPLAINTS CAN TURN INTO BIG PROBLEMS
44 YOU'VE GOT THE POWER
45 KEEP THE ROOM SMELL FRESH
46 MAKE SURE THAT THE PROBLEMS ARE SOLVED
47 DON'T HIDE THE PROBLEMS FROM YOUR MANAGER
48 BE SOLUTION ORIENTED
49 DON'T EVER FOOL THE GUESTS
50 DON'T MISGUIDE YOUR GUESTS
51 ORGANIZE DAILY DEPARTMENT MEETINGS
52 BE A TEAM PLAYER
53 HELP YOUR SPECIAL GUESTS WITH DISABILITIES
54 ACCOMPANY YOUR GUESTS
55 ANSWER THE PHONES AS QUICKLY AS POSSIBLE
56 DON'T USE YOUR SMARTPHONE FOR PERSONAL REASONS
57 VERIFY THE LUGGAGE
58 BE CAREFUL WITH THE FRAGILE STUFF
59 SEND THE GUEST LUGGAGE TO THEIR ROOM 7 MINUTES LATER
60 FOLLOW UP THE LOST LUGGAGE
61 LEARN TO ORCHESTRATE DIFFERENT PRIORITIES
62 SHARE THE DETAILS
63 HAVE SOME TOYS FOR THE KIDS
64 MAKE FAST CHECK-IN AND CHECK OUT
65 BE CREATIVE WITH EARLY CHECK-IN
66 GIVE THE INVOICE IN A FOLIO DURING CHECK-OUT
67 REMIND POTENTIALLY FORGOTTEN THINGS

68 GIVE THEM SOUVENIRS DURING THE CHECK-OUT
69 REVIEW BEFORE YOU ASSIGN THE ROOM
70 PAY ATTENTION TO ROOM CHANGES
71 ACCOMPANY AND PRESENT
72 BE A LOBBY AMBASSADOR
73 CHIT-CHAT WITH THE GUESTS AT THE END OF THE DAY
74 LET THE GUESTS KNOW ABOUT THE EVENTS IN TOWN
75 OFFER DISCOUNTS AND COUPONS
76 GIVE PRIZES FOR SHARING LOCATIONS
77 KNOW YOUR TOWN
78 GIVE A MAP
79 KNOW THE CURRENCY RATE
80 DON'T "HARD SELL" ANYTHING TO THE GUEST
81 WAKE UP CALL
82 MAKE LITTLE GESTURES AND OFFER LITTLE TREATS
83 BE RESOURCEFUL TO THE FAMILIES WITH CHILDREN
84 RESPECT COMES BEFORE THE TIP
85 BE READY FOR EMERGENCIES
86 KEEP IT CLEAN
87 PAY ATTENTION TO DND ROOMS!
88 SET THE ROOM TEMPERATURE WISELY
89 DON'T SPEAK LOUDLY
90 KEEP THE STAFF TROLLEYS AND HALLWAYS IN AN ORDER
91 KEEP READY A COMPLETE SET OF HOTEL GUEST
AMENITIES
92 HAVE A PILLOW MENU
93 PROVIDE TURNDOWN SERVICE
94 OFFER A GENEROUS ALL-YOU-CAN-EAT BUFFET
95 OFFER A RIGHT-PRICED AND ABUNDANT MENU
96 DO IT RIGHT: MINI BAR CHECKS
97 GUEST RELATIONS DEPARTMENT
98 PAY ATTENTION TO THE ALLERGIES
99 TAKE CARE OF YOUR PERSONAL APPEARANCE
100 PROVIDE EASY ACCESS TO INTERNET
101 MAKE YOUR HOTEL SAFE AND SECURE

ACKNOWLEDGMENTS

I'm eternally grateful to my valuable adviser Mr. Nikolay Tevekeliyski that I'm proud to have worked with, for being a great example with his understanding, human and moral values, to Mr. Serhan Öztas who shared his valuable experiences, devoted his precious time and tried his best to help me in my journey with patience and pleasure; and finally to my greatest chance in this life, my wife Özlem Avkan, who always trusted and supported me, and taught me the value of love and respect.

1

FALL IN LOVE WITH THIS JOB

We already knew when we were taking our first step to the hotel management that this job isn't about numbers, computations, or formulas. What we didn't know and learned throughout our experiences is that to do this job or make progress in this sector, the only way is to do it with LOVE. When you devote yourself with true love, this job requires sacrifices, persistence, and determination. It often requests the precious time you would spare for your whimsical lover, for your family or yourself.

2

BE READY TO EDUCATE

Education is a must! Oh, how often we use this classical phrase. Like hotel management, which has become a universal profession transcending the boundaries; the need for education is also a universal reality. Therefore, it's crucial for hotels to invest in the education and development of its staff. It is a must for staff to be motivated and always be open to learning. Training keeps you fit. In every period of your life; whichever job you have, whichever race you are in, wherever you live, you should always be open to change and education. Do not imprison yourself memorizing all the stereotypical methods of working. Any hotel making these mistakes, closing its doors to changes and innovations, will have to shut down its own doors one day complaining about redundancy

3

ORIENTATION FOR FASTER ADAPTATION

The process which we call as the complementary education is the orientation. The reason why the orientation differs from other training programs is that it examines the adaptation of new staff crew to the hotel operations closer. In this process, the participation in education, the capabilities of teamwork, and the personality of the new staff member are subjected to being tested. This process generally takes two days and has two stages. The first day is about explaining the structure, the character, the standards of the hotel, the techniques of problem-solving, and reminding the staff's responsibilities once again. The second day is for visiting all the departments of the hotel and meeting top-level managers in person. This short orientation program allows motivating the staff in adaptation.

4

IMPROVE YOUR LANGUAGE SKILLS

In the hospitality sector, whose universality is inevitable, we always face guests who come from every corner of the world. Usually, the common language of our guests, like in the whole world, is English. In the hospitality industry, proficiency in English is a must! Being fluent in English and adding another foreign language such as Spanish, Chinese, or French to your skill set, not only help you outstand, but also mean more earnings for you. Understanding guest's requests and being able to respond to them quickly is a must in this sector.

5

ALWAYS SMILE

What is smiling? It's expressing joy with the mimics of the face. Smiling is the gate to positive thoughts, enthusiasm, and tolerance. It increases the joy of life; it's good for physical health, and also gives peace and calm spiritually. It makes our approach to problems solution-oriented and increases our creativity. Smiling is free and contagious. Greeting and bidding farewell to the guests with a smiling face will make our guests remember the time passed in the hotel with a smiling face. Smiling is not only your essential tool in hospitality but also your biggest helper while solving the problems.

6

YOUR MOOD AND ENERGY
SHOULD BE HIGH

Imagine yourself as an athlete preparing for the Olympics. In the Olympics, you have only one chance to prove yourself to the world. Now, the customer and guest service requires that you live that day every day. Being fit and keeping your mood high brings guest satisfaction to a high level: Not sleeping very well relying on young age, not eating well, and adding the bad habits like drinking and smoking, waste a lot of your power already. When you add personal issues, it's barely possible imagining to run for the Olympics, right? We have to be careful with our lifestyle and leave all the problems behind when we come to the hotel and wear our uniform. Otherwise, we will fail.

7

GREET YOUR GUESTS IN A WARM WAY

Guest satisfaction starts with the greeting at the door and continues until bidding farewell. Our number one goal for guest satisfaction is this rule, and also it's one of the essential practices in hospitality. We already mentioned the importance of smiling, being energetic, and having high morale. It'll do more than okay to greet our guests tired of traveling. We have to show them how grateful we are because they chose us and also make them think about how lucky they are because they preferred us. I had witnessed guests who are upset to leave when their departure day came because of the established warm relations. We should see them off saying "See you again."

8

ADDRESS YOUR GUESTS WITH THEIR NAME

Addressing your guests with their name does not only honor them but also brings quality and professionalism to your hotel. While the Doorman or Bellboy make the first encounter, they should start addressing the guests with the name —if it's written- on their luggage. The guest that is accompanied to the reception should be presented to the reception staff with his name, and this chain of professionalism must go on and on. Many departments in the hotel have the opportunity to address the guests with their name. How is it possible? The housekeeping department can see it on the floor report and address the guest with their name every morning when they knock on their door. The technical service crew who checks all the floors and intervenes when there's a problem also has to carry this list with them. You can learn the name of your guest from the different sources in the hotel; it can be a room or a reservation number. Addressing the guests with their names will make them feel distinguished.

9

DON'T BE AFRAID TO INTRODUCE YOURSELF

I take joy in presenting myself and giving cards. I recommend to every hotel staff that has direct contact with the guest, like the waiter who serves in a la carte restaurant or housekeeper who knocks on the doors for cleaning, to learn how to do this and to get joy from doing it. Imagine the moment of the arrival of a guest; first, a warm welcome, addressing with his name and "Mr. Brown... Thank you. My name is Jack. For all your needs during your stay, you can contact me by pressing 0 from the phone in your room, and reach us 24 hours." The housekeeper who cleans the room can say, "Mr. Brown, my name is Laila, I will be serving your room during your stay." These phrases make your guests very happy and bring out your service quality.

10

BE THANKFUL

Thanking someone is an art of showing contentment, and you should perform this art. You can win people's heart; turn the negative into positive and souring faces to positive smiles in an instant by only thanking them. Thanking doesn't cost anything; you can multiply it as you wish. When you thank not only your guests but also your colleagues, this effect will be contagious. Be thankful. Thank your guests for preferring you after a long and tiring trip they made. Thank your colleagues for not leaving you alone against demanding guests and seeking solutions together with you. Thank them.

11

PEOPLE LEAVE BUT

QUALITY STAYS

Quality, in its core meaning, is to satisfy the needs of your guests. Quality starts with applying the standards specified by your hotel. These standards have the characteristics of law, and each staff member has to oblige. You must have heard of some of these phrases a lot, "the place that I had dinner was very high quality" or "the place that I stayed was very high quality." What makes a hotel high quality is the staff member that works in it, and the most crucial reason why your guests prefer your hotel is the quality. You should give quality service so that the efficiency of your hotel rises, its costs diminish, and high occupancy rates display a continuity. Quality lets everyone win.

12

BE ADAPTABLE

An adaptable person is the one who adapts to change and can learn quickly and who isn't afraid of the new. The hotel which has to renew itself constantly must also have staff that is innovative and adaptable. In addition to fulfilling the different requests of different sort of guests, staff members should also be creative, and understanding their deficiencies, seeing their mistakes beforehand. Staff members must produce ideas about the work they do and suggest them to the management. It's tough to attain lasting success without a productive staff. A person who works after a training program will have ideas about what to improve and how to improve it. Each staff member needs to put his improvement ideas into practice after training and have a creative, solution-oriented approach that builds up guest satisfaction.

13

BE PATIENT AND UNDERSTANDING

Your guests, whether they have come a long way or not, are a wide range of colorful people who have different cultures and lifestyles. We may not know their mood or what their expectations will be during their accommodation. Only when problems emerge that we realize some necessities. In the hospitality business, there will be people who will rant about their problem to you, irritate you, or even come on you, like the heartbreaking ones who think they have every right to exploit you.

For this reason, always be patient and understanding to your guests; this isn't only valid for guests but also valid for your colleagues. If you can make this happen, you can make everything happen.

14

EMPATHIZE

Empathy, in other sense, understanding, is putting yourself in other's place and understanding their emotions. It's a trait that we need to develop in our daily life as well as in hotel management. When an angry person thinks that he can't express himself very well, he will only get more upset. Telling your angry guest that you understand and share his feelings will comfort him. It's one of the most important approaches to dealing with the problems of our guests. Many successful hotels continuously organize training programs to increase the empathy of their staff.

15

NEVER DESPISE YOUR GUESTS

It's foremost yours and then your team's priority to fulfill the needs of your guests. You absolutely should not despise them. What does it mean to despise? Let's analyze this word. Despise comes from the Latin word "dēspiciō", "dē" meaning "down" and "speciō" meaning "I look at". When the two words emerge, it means looking down on somebody. We must never let our guests feel this way. They are the ones adding value to our hotel's existence, forming our standards of working, living and succeeding. We must do whatever we can not to make them feel despised.

16

GET RID OF YOUR EGO

Ego means "I" by a simple definition. A person who thinks of himself, prioritize himself, talks about his qualifications is called an egoist. The biggest obstacle to teamwork and cooperation is the fact that the individuals see themselves isolated from the team and think in a manner that prioritizes themselves. That's not a good foundation for hotel management. We should give importance to teamwork and harmony. We should not only help our department but also help whenever any other busy department needs it. Getting rid of your ego, minimizing the usage of "I" will give you a different perspective on both hotel management and your life, which is the key to success.

17

DON'T DISRESPECT

My dear colleagues, "respect" may mean something different for each person. My comment on respect with the experience that I had in hotel management is: "The sense of hesitation and an invisible boundary." Making every guest feel at home without disturbing them. First, this is the right of our guests who chose our place to stay, and second, the right of our colleagues. You should respect every private moment and every need of your guest during their accommodation. Primarily, this is a delicate matter for the staff entering guests' room. Everything that you see should stay with you.

Orkun Avkan

18

DON'T BE A RACIST

Since the title is crystal-clear, I'll keep it short this time. The universal hotel industry tells us not to discriminate guests because of their color, language, religion, race, country. In the hotel as well as in our daily life, this subject isn't open to discussion. A careless act of the employee can cause significant damage to our hotel and the employee.

19

DON'T PICK GUESTS TO SERVE

Maybe one of the biggest mistakes is picking guests to serve. This mistake that I witnessed mostly in front-office and food & beverage departments causes serious troubles and discomfort of the other guests. As you might already know, there are several types of rooms at hotels. Acting in a particular manner to the guests staying in luxury rooms like royal suites or to the guests staying in more modest rooms isn't acceptable. Likewise, serving and behaving differently to the guests who tip well and who doesn't tip is a form of discrimination. It's a big mistake. Any person preferring your hotel and coming in becomes your guest and deserves your service in an equal manner. Each guest is important to you. You can never know what benefits they can bring to your hotel.

20

GUESTS FIRST

In the 18th rule, we talked about respect. We can think of this rule as complimentary to respect. Let me explain what it means by examples: When you greet your guests at the main entrance, the priority is them. No matter how urgent your situation is, don't enter before them. Another issue that we have a lot of complaints about guest satisfaction is using the guests' elevator. When the doors of the elevator open, we should wait for our guests to exit. Even when you share the elevator, you should first look for what floor your guest wants to go and always give priority to them. The reason is apparent; you're using the guest elevator. Accompanying your guest in the elevator to their floor is essential to show our quality service and professionalism.

21

LEARN THE STANDARDS OF THE HOTEL

It's one of the essential matters to maximize guest satisfaction. Every hotel should define its standards and train accordingly to create a team spirit in employees, to make their approach solution-oriented and to strengthen the communication between the departments. The standards are the details on the road to perfection. Certain standards like the hotel guest amenities, the technique of making beds, the style of answering the phone calls and the room service should be established and applied. Any hotel that doesn't have standards is on a hiding to nothing.

Great Hotel Service

52

22

COMFORT YOUR GUESTS

The first need of the guest who preferred our hotel is to stay with a warm smile and a sense of comfort. Relaxing is the primary purpose of our guests anyway. For example, the guest who comes to check-in has a doubt in his mind: "Is there any problem with my reservation?" If you tell your new guest upon his arrival: "Mr. Brown, we were expecting you." You can observe from his body language and attitude that he is very much relieved. The "Check-in" isn't only giving room keys. You should repeat the reservation details to our guest and get their confirmation so that our guests know what is waiting for them during their check-out. Comforting your valuable guests is essential.

23

GIVE THE CORRECT INFORMATION ON THE MEDIA

Misinformation or obsolete information is the primary source of complaints. You can be sure that everyone who makes a reservation examines the facilities of the hotel in detail. There are even people memorizing them. Any information that doesn't reflect the truth or any wrong information will become a problem for us later. Exaggerating the size (square meter/ft.) of the rooms, adding some facilities that don't exist, not letting the guests profit from the discount advantages will disappoint our guests that make comparisons after. This situation that happens upon arrival to the hotel will cause distrust and disputes that even go as far as requesting refunds. Don't trigger dissatisfaction of your guests at the first moment. Always be honest with your guests.

24

PRICE IN A CONSISTENT WAY

While evaluating the hotels to stay, the guests check the price first. The guests want to see if the amount is worth for the service offered. I am well aware of the sales policies of hotels, but the lack of alternatives for big organizations and conferences and thus raising prices, even if it increases the income of the hotel in short-term, in the bigger picture, it is a critical problem making the guests question the hotel's reliability. This sales policy will upset your regular guests or the people visiting for touristic purposes in the long term, and make your hotel undesirable. In addition to the transformation of a short-term income to a long-term loss, it won't be surprising if your hotel ratings drop in online marketplaces and your hotel gets negative reviews.

25

INFORM BY AN EMAIL

We already explained how important the information on the website is in the 23rd rule. In online markets, it's always the top priority to ensure trust. The guests often have doubts about making the right reservations. Even if the automatic responding email is comforting most of the times, sending a "WELCOME" email as the Guest Relations department, and providing information about the hotel and its surroundings will be very useful.

Additionally, you can also offer an airport transfer to your guests who recently made their reservations. You can send a welcome message and the location of the hotel by an online tool. In this case, the guests can quickly contact you if they have any problems.

26

RESPOND TO THE REVIEWS

The comments on the online platforms for your hotel show the shortcomings that you don't realize. The rating system in online pages and complaint forms in the rooms for guest satisfaction are precious feedbacks. A lot of guests prefer writing their thoughts instead of telling them in person. You should respond to all reviews, good or bad from your guests. Each comment is a second chance for you to make it correct. Thank your guests for the comments they leave and show how valuable they are by responding to them. Don't leave any comment unanswered. You may not change a negative review, but you can make your guest prefer you in the future.

27

UNDERSTAND THE REQUESTS PROACTIVELY

When you analyze the requests before they occur, when you are as sharp as a needle, you create a smart and flowing work stream. Think about a guest with his child in a restaurant. After giving the menu, your first job is to take the order of the child and fulfill it as soon as possible; this will always come up in food & beverage standards. The reason for this is that the children get hungry quicker, and they tend to act in a manner that causes difficult situations for their parents. Maybe their initial thought is to feed their child first. In cases like this, always remind your guest that you're working for their comfort, and their requests are critical to you.

28

DON'T SAY IT'S NOT MY JOB

In the hospitality business, we're here to support each other and make up for our shortcomings. For guest satisfaction, every department needs each other. We should run to help other teams without considering a personal gain. If we say "Every department is responsible for itself," we prepare not only our end but also the end of our hotel. Let me explain the situation with a simple example: You saw an empty cup on the coffee table in the lobby or noticed a piece of garbage on the floor, which may not be relevant to your duty. Ignoring this cup or trash in front of your eyes is against your business vision. How much time can it take for you to notice and take the initiative for it? These split-second decisions are the essence of the hospitality business, and they will take you ahead in teamwork. Thus, it will raise guest satisfaction.

29

AVOID CONFLICTS BETWEEN YOUR PERSONAL LIFE AND YOUR JOB

Whatever you experience outside of the hotel, in your private life or with your colleagues at the hotel, none of your guests have to put up with your caprice, your anger or your grumpiness. Never forget that. The moment you come to work, you put all your troubles in your locker and start to give the service your guests paid for. Take care of your problems by yourself and don't bring them to your job as a burden and lower the service quality for your guests and colleagues, don't ever let that happen. If you can't fix the problem what you need to do is going to your department's manager and telling him that you can't work that day. This solution will be the best choice for everyone.

30

USE YOUR

BODY LANGUAGE WELL

Your body language has a vital role in communication. According to research, while the power of the words we use have 7% effectiveness, the power of body language is 55%. Although your voice has 38% effectiveness, it isn't as much as your body language. Moreover, the best reflection of the thoughts and emotions is body language. You must improve your body language. Remind yourself that the foundation of a reassuring communication for guest satisfaction is the body language.

31

DON'T MAKE PROMISES THAT YOU CAN'T KEEP

Consider a situation when it is impossible to keep your promise. For example, you're working at the reception, and you promised a room change to an unsatisfied guest, and you couldn't keep this promise. How does it make your guests feel? You made a promise to help, and you couldn't keep it. This promise that you couldn't keep will firstly harm you, then your guest and your hotel. So, don't make any promises that you can't keep; try to find alternative solutions. This rule is crucial not only in the hospitality industry but also in your private life.

32

NEVER SAY NO

TO YOUR GUESTS

Are you aware of the problems that come with saying "NO" to the guests? This word is negativity that disinclines your guests, making them think of never coming back again. The word "No" is easy for you, but it's not easy for your guests to accept. If you need to give negative answers, you should use words like "Sorry," "Unfortunately," "I can't make that happen, but I can suggest this to you" etc. While using these phrases, you explain the impossibility of the request without hurting them. If you need to use these expressions, always try to find a better alternative.

33

USE MAGICAL EXPRESSIONS: "CERTAINLY, SURE, WITH PLEASURE"

We've just examined how the word "No" can be misunderstood and cause problems. Employee responses define their quality. The employees should use the right words and avoid giving answers that may lead to misunderstandings. The way to do this is to use these magical words: "Certainly," "Sure," "With Pleasure." Do not hesitate to use these words; they will bring quality to you and your hotel.

34

DON'T BECOME FRIENDS WITH THE GUESTS

Becoming friends with the guests is one of the biggest mistakes that we make. From the moment you become friends with your guests, you'll start trying to fulfill every request of the guests because we try to do every favor for our friends. Their number of requests won't decrease, and even they will be more requesting. This situation leads to breaking the rules and standards of the hotel. Let me tell you one of my colleagues' latest experiences. The guest buys some food from the supermarket to have a special recipe soup made for him in the restaurant. One of my colleagues is close to him; he can't say no to the guest. The next day the guest comes with some new food from the supermarket to have another special meal made for him. This situation isn't acceptable. In this situation, you gave someone an inch, and he'll take a yard. You should be aware of the boundaries between the guest and employee before it's too late.

35

RESPECT THE GUESTS' PRIVATE LIFE

"What happens in hotel stays in the hotel." Never forget this phrase. Everything that happens from the moment our guest arrives at the hotel, and the moment they leave should stay private. Every employee should pay attention to this matter. For example, we never share the guest's accommodation details with third parties, or we don't tell about the personal belongings that we see at their room during their accommodation. Please note that the slightest information sharing might turn into a severe and legal problem.

36

DON'T TALK ABOUT YOUR PRIVATE LIFE

This rule is merely being disrespectful to the guest. As we already said, don't be friends with them and don't share your private life as well. While the guests prefer your hotel to get away from their busy life and distress, listening to your problems is not at all pleasant. For example, I witness from time to time housekeeping staff pile on the agony of their private life to get a little more tip from servicing the rooms. This situation not only harms your business but also is a big minus for the professionalism of your hotel.

37

RESPECT INCOGNITO

In the hotel management jargon, the word "Incognito," means not disturbing the guest during their accommodation. What makes this rule different than the 35th rule is the privacy of the current guest. For example, we apply "Incognito" for the guest who comes to the front office and requests not to be disturbed. In this case, we don't connect a phone line to the guests' room; housekeeping members can't enter; however, when the guest asks again, these services become active again. Please take this matter seriously; otherwise, you can have serious complaints.

38

HELP TO CELEBRATE SPECIAL DAYS OF YOUR GUESTS

For many people, the hotel becomes not only a place to sleep but also a place to come together as a family on a special day. Small gestures on special days of guests can go a long way. It can be a birthday organization or an anniversary of engagement/marriage. Surprises like room decorations, special treats, and beautiful champagne can conquer hearts. It's our job to leave a trace on the lives of our guests. Never forget that it's in your hands to add something special to the lives of your guests.

39

COMMUNICATE EFFECTIVELY

Always keep good communications with your guests. Don't hesitate to say "I'm here for you" so that they don't hesitate to contact you when they have a problem. In this case, you get the chance to make your guests speak up about their problems and to solve their problem before they leave. You may not be the genie in the lamp, but you can make a difference with your approach. Encourage your guest to share their experiences; listen to them empathically, and try to solve their problems with your heart and mind.

40

CHEAP PRODUCT EXPENSIVE COMPLAINT

This matter is especially relevant to the purchasing department. Usually, purchasing department decides to seek low-cost or less expensive products with the instructions from the management. Unfortunately, this effort results in most of the time badly. The most evident example of searching for cheap happens in all-you-can-eat buffet breakfasts. One of the essential services is breakfast. The breakfast should always be fresh, varied, and vibrant. Don't cut corners in an all-you-can-eat buffet. The road to the heart goes from the stomach. Always remember that.

41

WATCH OUT FOR OPPORTUNITIES TO DO GOOD THINGS

My dear colleagues, the essence of our job is the satisfaction of our guests, never forget that. For this reason, you should pay the utmost attention to your surroundings. That means you have to sense your guests' needs at any moment and fulfill them. For example, if you see a guest with a baby stroller, you need to open the door for them to make a smooth exit. The guest comes from shopping at the end of the day, and they have some bags in their hands. You need to offer help immediately to carry their shopping bags; and if your guest doesn't accept your help, you need to accompany them, call the elevator and help them get on the elevator. That's what we call a service opportunity.

42

KNOW YOUR GUEST

Everyone has a routine of habits, requests, and rules in this life. Learning and respecting them is between our primary objectives. Observe their daily routines well to make our hotel's guests comfortable. You should note to their profiles particular foods they prefer, the type of pillow they choose, their newspaper choice, their hobbies and phobias, the details like whether they have an allergy or not. When they revisit us, you should be prepared for their requests before they even ask; this is an essential step to guest satisfaction.

43

LITTLE COMPLAINTS CAN TURN INTO BIG PROBLEMS

Thinking that the complaints you receive from the guests are not important or insignificant will become massive problems for us later on. This situation starts when you don't take the complaints of your guests seriously. "Not caring" might be the number one on the not to do list during your guest's accommodation period. The first impression of a newly arrived guest who preferred our hotel is formed by the service, the caring and the attitude of the staff; then the guest realizes other details like the location, the comfort and the cleanliness of the hotel. In order not to add a new mistake to your mistakes, you should take care of the expressed problems with great interest and seriousness. Remember that every problem you don't deal with will cause your hotel to lose money.

44

YOU'VE GOT THE POWER

There is a "Guest Relations" department in the hotels to communicate with the guests to solve their problems. The primary objective of this department is to provide the necessary communication with the other departments to solve the problems of unsatisfied guests. But, is the guest relation department enough to solve the guest problems? Of course not. Each staff member should support this department as they are authorized to solve the problems. Any department that comes across a problem has to tell about the problem to the head of their department and the Guest Relations department as well. Don't forget that the best way to solve the problems is to communicate.

45

KEEP THE ROOM SMELL FRESH

It's one of the most received complaints. As you already know, the hotel rooms are separated as smoking and non-smoking. We even divide them into floors. The reason why we do is that the smell of the tobacco and similar products disturbs the guests and triggers asthmatic attacks. If a room smells very badly because of cigarettes, we leave the window open and make the cleaning at the last step. The control of this type of rooms should be made by the floor managers carefully. If you decide that the smell is too hard to deal with, you should use the ozone generating equipment. If you use ozone generating equipment, wait 15-20 minutes, air the room, and finally use the conditioner. If the guest is still in the room never use ozone generating equipment. Nobody wants to stay in a smelly room, even if they also smoke.

46

MAKE SURE THAT THE
PROBLEMS ARE SOLVED

Throughout the last couple of rules, we dwelled on the solutions of the guest problems, how essential they are, and the consent of the guests to solve these problems. Learning about the result is also important after all the efforts. You have the chance to determine if their problem was solved and if you satisfied them when they're leaving the hotel. After the guest leaves the hotel, there's nothing much you can do later; this is the last step and should be taken care of before the guest leaves. Whichever department the guest had problems with, the reception must ask how was their accommodation. If there are still unsolved issues, we should tell about them to the Guest Relations, and take the last initiative at this moment. Don't miss your last chance.

47

DON'T HIDE THE PROBLEMS FROM YOUR MANAGER

This is a common mistake. Hiding the unintentional mistakes that you make from your managers is a dead-end street taken together. Your managers don't get angry at you because of the mistakes you make, but the mistakes you don't tell. If you hide these mistakes, no one can correct. Of course, there is a solution to the mistakes you make. Your department managers will show you how to fix them. Your department managers have to know about the problems. Never do something behind your manager's back; share your mistakes.

48

BE SOLUTION ORIENTED

You might have challenging problems to solve. You can be out of breath and without solution while trying to fulfill your guests' requests. Of course, you'll have unsatisfied, selfish, and even freeloader guests. Don't let it discourage you. Your approach should always be solution-oriented. Always offer things that you can do for them; try to find common grounds as much as possible.

49

DON'T EVER FOOL THE GUESTS

Never forget this rule and never even think about it. When you're in this situation, nobody can save you. For example; from time to time, the hotels become short on room types, and front office department tells a white lie to save the day. They offer a different room type as the type the guest requested. But a lie never lives to be old. When the guest asks another employee about the room type the next day, the truth comes out. This mistake cost a lot. When you fool a guest, you don't have any chance to correct it. You will pay the cost later.

50

DON'T MISGUIDE YOUR GUESTS

You must know about everything in your hotel. You should prepare yourself for the questions that your guests might ask and guiding them well should be your priority. For example, you must know and spa & fitness location. Every employee should have the answers to the questions about their hotel. Misguiding the guests and not being able to answer their questions are not well received by them at all. The education programs which we call "refreshment" classes should be given every three months and any change at the hotel should be shared with the employees.

51

ORGANIZE DAILY DEPARTMENT MEETINGS

The departmental meeting is a crucial step to healthy communication. Each department should evaluate the previous day and essential topics such as inconveniences, positive developments, VIP guests, the numbers of arrivals and departures, the banquet organizations, in short, evaluate the general operation and have a grasp. Each staff should be prepared for everything before they start their shift and take the necessary precautions. This type of meetings should be obligatory in the department. We can also consider this rule as the first step towards guest satisfaction.

52

BE A TEAM PLAYER

The team is the name given to a specific group of people who have different talents and work in harmony as a whole to meet some objectives and purposes. With teamwork, the individuals try continuously to minimize the problems and their mistakes. I want to talk about this by giving the example of our own body. We all must have experienced how a malfunction of any organ in our body affects all our system. Indeed, what we need to do is work as a team, find common grounds approaching the problems and events to solve them. If we become a team with the necessary communication, everyone's job will be a lot easier.

53

HELP YOUR SPECIAL GUESTS WITH DISABILITIES

We accommodate guests from every corner of the world; old ones, the ones having trouble to walk or the ones with any other condition. If a specific type of guests visits our hotel, we must certainly inform the other departments. During their accommodation, the responsible housekeeper should pay close attention to their needs. Especially during the cleaning of their rooms, it's a courtesy to have a Guest Relations member there. Always make their stay comfortable for your guests. It's essential always to have a wheelchair where the Guest Service members can reach easily. With our quick action, we can conquer hearts.

Great Hotel Service

54

ACCOMPANY YOUR GUESTS

You should know about the plan of the lobby and the halls of your hotel, which might seem like a labyrinth to your guests. I'm sure you have other significant things to do that your manager asked from you. But it won't take hours to help your guests while they're trying to find a place in the hotel. Accompanying your guests for 6-10 seconds will help your guests find the place they want to go and bring out your hotel's quality. As we always say, add value and make them feel special.

55

ANSWER THE PHONES AS QUICKLY AS POSSIBLE

There is no end to domestic or international calls to your hotel. They will even contact you from their room if they have any needs. What matters here is that you answer the incoming call at least within the third ring. Another rule is responding correctly to the requests in a short period of time. You must have a well-adjusted tone of voice, fluent speaking pace, and the capacities to listen and understand the other party. Otherwise, you can keep the line busy, and you might be late to answer the next call; this results in guest dissatisfaction.

56

DON'T USE YOUR SMARTPHONE FOR PERSONAL REASONS

Even if we live in the era of technology, the increasing effect of technology in our life should not be a reason to lose control and disrespect others. Use your cell phone just as much as your job requires it to use. Never make phone calls around your guests and check social media; this is rude behavior. I've seen a lot of staff who doesn't take care of the guests while looking at their phone; this can even cause financial loss, cast doubt on our hotel's professional stance and harm it.

57

VERIFY THE LUGGAGE

During the check-in and check-out of our guests, when we are taking their luggage to the storage room, always verify their luggage and look after them. The problems with the luggage might give you lots of headaches. Some of these problems are; the stuff that is forgotten in the vehicle, the things that the guests forget to take, the forgotten stuff in the hotel, confusing the bags and theft. In this case, the hotel is responsible, and it might get very vexing. It's a must to use a Luggage Log Book to be able to control this. We must register the guest's name, their room, the date they give and the day they will take back the luggage, the name of the person that gives and takes it back and how many pieces there are. The only way to minimize the problems is protecting the luggage, providing good communication between doorman and the bellboy; this will relieve you and also ease the workflow.

58

BE CAREFUL WITH THE FRAGILE STUFF

We talked about taking care of the luggage and stuff in the storage in the previous rule. If we don't treat in a sensitive manner the luggage we carry or protect, looking after them doesn't mean anything. Nobody wants to see that their stuff is damaged after a long road trip. For this reason, primarily the Doorman and the Bellboy should pay the necessary attention to it. We must always ask about the potential fragile stuff in the luggage to our guests. After this question, the fragile stuff has to be put at the top or separately. Another tip to ease this process is the "Fragile" sticker. It is attached by the hotel and lets the other people be more careful about it.

59

SEND THE GUEST LUGGAGE TO THEIR ROOM 7 MINUTES LATER

When you're done with the check-in process, one of the guys from the Guest Service will accompany the guest to their room. Here, the Guest Service team should tighten the reins. After the guests enter their room, their luggage should be sent in 7 minutes. Why 7 minutes? Because, primarily, after a long road trip the guests tend to use the toilets. From my experiences, I can tell that they can be busy for 2 or 4 minutes. It wouldn't be so great to catch your guests while they are using the toilets. We should give them the necessary time and space.

60

FOLLOW UP THE LOST LUGGAGE

There can always be small errors in a world where easy and fast transportation is promised with the advancing technology. Asking our guests during the Check-in process if they have any lost luggage shows that we care about them. If they have lost luggage, you should take responsibility for the follow-up. Let their guests have their vacation in their limited time and not ruin their day dealing with lost baggage. The reception team must have lost luggage forms beside them.

61

LEARN TO ORCHESTRATE DIFFERENT PRIORITIES

Sometimes our duties might be overwhelming. Responding to all the expectations becomes very difficult, and the problems are likely to occur. While the receptionist is busy with check-in and check-out procedures of the guests, dealing with external calls might cause delays in processing time and deprivation of the guests from necessary services. Prolongation of the processing time in urgent situations might get intolerable, and you can get a massive reaction from your guests. You'd better be prepared for it. First and last impressions are the most indelible parts to consider revisiting. If the receptionist has to do the duties of a switchboard operator, he has to provide fluent telephone traffic while taking care of the requests fast.

62

SHARE THE DETAILS

From the moment we confirm the reservations of our guests, we should start comforting them and share some details while asking questions. The necessary details should be noted in order not to have any problems during the accommodation and check-out. Primary subjects are clarifying the check-out date, payment type, taking the invoice address if available, etc. You can vary these questions according to the standards of your hotel. Verifying the details like this not only provides you ease in operation but also gives the reassurance to the guests that their accommodation will be hassle-free.

63

HAVE SOME TOYS

FOR THE KIDS

Imagine a family coming to the reception to check-in. There are two possibilities for the behavior of kids. The first one is that they run and play until they become breathless; the second one is seeking attention while climbing to the reception desk beside their parents. In these cases which require urgent action, your approach should be affectionate and caring. Always prioritize the kids and lessen the burden on their parents. Find temporary activities for them according to their age. You can stall and entertain them with a remote controlled car, an unfinished puzzle, a Barbie doll or simple mind games. If you make this move, you will get the appreciation of the family and conquer their hearts.

64

MAKE FAST CHECK-IN AND CHECK OUT

In the 62nd rule, we mentioned that we need to verify the details of their accommodation during the check-in process. This rule is a follow-up on that rule. The guests want these two procedures to be taken care of quickly. Check-in must last maximum of 3 minutes and 10 seconds; check-out must be below 2 minutes and 50 seconds. The check-out process starts when the guest calls the reception from their room. In this case, we ask them how many bags they have and if they need any transportation. Then, we direct the mini bar staff to the room. If there are too many bags, the Bellboy should head to the room with a trolley. If he doesn't take the trolley, he will lose a lot of time. Getting information about their transportation needs beforehand enables you to take the necessary precautions in the case of rush hours, and possible cases of not finding any taxi.

65

BE CREATIVE WITH EARLY CHECK-IN

We call the guests who come before their scheduled check-in time as "Early check-in." Many hotels have their specific schedules for the check-in and check-out operations. These hours may vary. If the hotel is too busy the day before check-in, the guests who come early might have to wait for their room. In this case, we should help our early guests. You can take their luggage to the storage room; offer them breakfast, a tea, or a cup of coffee, a shower, and a chance to change their clothes if you have a spa area. You can give information about what to visit in the city and even arrange tours for them. If they are out visiting the city, you should call and inform them when their room is ready.

66

GIVE THE INVOICE IN A FOLIO DURING CHECK-OUT

Lately, the Front Office staff wants to make quick check-outs, but then they realize their mistakes, and these mistakes go even as far as requesting the invoice back from the guests. In this case, the accounting department is boiling with anger. Print an informative folio during the check out of our guests and make the original invoice come out correctly by explaining the details. It's always a troublesome issue to make changes after the guests check the folio or the invoice. This nuisance brings big problems to the company employees and goes as far as cutting from the salary. It also creates a negative impression like: "I've stayed at that hotel, and they couldn't even make out an invoice correctly." Let's accept it; it isn't a nice impression at all.

67

REMIND POTENTIALLY FORGOTTEN THINGS

According to research, the most forgotten things by the guests are mobile phones and laptop battery chargers. Ask your guests during their check-out if they picked their personal belongings from the safe in the rooms and their battery chargers. This question puts a bug in their ear. Upon hearing this question, every guest will need to go through or go back to their rooms and check. These questions also lighten the Lost & Found department's burden. Housekeeping department must do their part in this issue. When the guest leaves the room for the check-out, the maid or the supervisor should check the room. We shouldn't forget to check also the safe box. This routine check also enables us to find a solution before the guest leaves if the room is damaged in any way.

68

GIVE THEM SOUVENIRS DURING THE CHECK-OUT

We should ask during the check out if the guest had any problems during their accommodation. The primary purpose of these questions is to make them tell us the problems and have a second chance to fix it if there are any. If everything is going well, give them a little souvenir in the meantime. I think a fridge magnet is handy. If you ask why, whenever they see this magnet on their fridge, they will think about their memories and you. You can also use the products like a little soap, a locally handcrafted item, or a key chain as a souvenir. Feel free to give souvenirs.

69

REVIEW BEFORE YOU ASSIGN THE ROOM

Again a crucial rule, assigning the rooms after checking the reservations, that is to say after backup check. While assigning the rooms, we review the requests of the guests with the information of room type, how many people they are, the need of a baby bed or an extra bed according to the age of their children if they have, the preference of specific rooms like smoking or non-smoking and high floor rooms. Of course, it isn't that easy to assign the rooms. For example; while you're assigning a room when a guest is still in there, in the case of an extension request for a few days, it causes the change of assignments and even goes as far as changing the rooms of the guest staying currently. For this reason, the person assigning the rooms must also check the following dates before assigning the rooms.

70

PAY ATTENTION TO ROOM CHANGES

Many of the guests come to request a room change in the following day of their accommodation. Some of the reasons for this are the noise, not being able to settle, the size of the room, its location, the view, and the comfort of the bed. Front office members might not like these types of requests justifiably. Let me tell you how many departments we give burden to when we allow this operation. Of course, firstly the Guest Service department comes into the room for moving their luggage. For housekeeping, it's a nuisance to deal with a room change while they have all the check-outs in their hands, and also it's a loss of time and money when they have to change all the sheets and beddings again. Then the mini bar staff comes to the action, and the technique service follows to check if there is any problem, and after that, the Front Office staff does the paperwork for the room change. I'm sure our guests also don't want this troublesome and lasting process. You must ask the guests if they like their room during their check-in to avoid the cases of changes later.

71

ACCOMPANY AND PRESENT

When the check-in process is over, we give the room key to our guest and the Guest Relations or the Guest Service is introduced to the guest to accompany them. If there is any, we verify the belongings of the guest. It's important to accompany our guests and introduce them the different Outlets of the hotel. These Outlets are sections like the lobby, the breakfast restaurant, the a la carte restaurant, spa & fitness, business center, and hairdresser. Paying attention to this matter will profit us because of two crucial reasons. First, for the adaptation of our guest to the hotel and second, making extra profits by introducing the outlets.

72

BE A LOBBY AMBASSADOR

Who is this Lobby Ambassador? Ambassador is the ambassador we know; the term lobby ambassador is used to describe the managers of different departments standing in the lobby and the general areas of the hotel in turns for a period. While they stand, their title changes briefly. The reason why they stand in the lobby is apparent. They greet the guests and see them off, communicate with the guests, ask if they had any problems during their accommodation or not. Thus they try to find fast solutions to the problems. They report the issues and solutions to the General Manager.

73

CHIT-CHAT WITH THE GUESTS AT THE END OF THE DAY

Having strong communication with your guests is indispensable. If you catch your tired guests at the end of the day worn to the bone because of traveling all day or working their fingers to the bone, make a little conversation without disturbing them. If the conversation goes on, treat them a cup of coffee. These chats will make them think about their good memories of the day and let them relive their experiences on their vacation. You will even have the chance for closer communication because they are sharing their memories with you.

74

LET THE GUESTS KNOW ABOUT THE EVENTS IN TOWN

Our guests will have their schedule of accommodation set before they arrive. They may have a vacation plan or a business plan; there can always be changes in their programs. Your guidance and ideas will increase their joy of the trip, and let them experience different things. That's the reason why you need to know about the events, the museums, the art galleries and places like these in town. Wrong advice of yours can cause the guest to waste their precious time. Nobody has a minute to waste.The most valuable thing is time; remember that.

75

OFFER DISCOUNTS AND COUPONS

In the 71st rule, we mentioned how important it is to accompany the guest to their room and other hotel outlets. During this moment, presenting our guest's privileges, giving them discount cards will let them pass a better time and allow our hotel to profit more. Telling them about the fact that they can benefit from the quality service of the hotel with discounts provides a unique experience for our guests. These little discounts you make will become the reason why they will prefer you next time. The opportunities and smiling faces will remain in their minds.

76

GIVE PRIZES FOR SHARING LOCATIONS

Now in the 21st century, everyone has a smartphone. Everyone can share or follow ideas simultaneously on social media. The platforms such as Facebook, Twitter, and Instagram are pioneers of this era, which allow us to share our thoughts and photos without having to be a professional photographer or a writer. Liking the guest's shared locations from the official social media account of our hotel and responding with little gifts are always positive. The gestures we make in this era where we can reach thousands of people with our fingertip can make a positive impact on our hotel in social media.

77

KNOW YOUR TOWN

You always need to guide your guests correctly about the city and events, whether they're tourist or businessman, whether they come from abroad or they are domestic. We can list the information we need as; museums, art galleries, historical places, shopping malls, places of entertainment, theatre, cinema, and public transportation. The bad news is, their questions might not be limited to these. We must know the area and the city we live in and develop ourselves. Imagine a tourist asking about something you don't know about your city. Or even better, don't imagine, start searching and learning.

78

GIVE A MAP

On the previous rule, we mentioned the importance of knowing your town. We said that our potential guests might prefer us for business or vacation purposes. Even in the age of smartphones, a traditional paper map still makes sense because it is larger. Make sure that you give them a map during their check-in or at least offer them. You need to mark the location details on the map.

For this reason, you need to know the historical places, museums, art galleries, entertainment places, or activity centers for kids, metro stops, and even ferry ports. Mastering the map isn't only crucial for Front Office department, but other departments need to be able to answer these questions as well.

79

KNOW THE CURRENCY RATE

One of the most challenging subjects for our guests is naturally calculating the currencies. Informing the guests about this subject is also our duty. A list of current currency rates that we can show during their check-in or a fixed rate can help our guests make the calculations easier. This way, you avoid our guests making undesirable expenses. The guests making correct calculations can act confidently, and this is one of the most important things that you can provide.

Orkun Avkan

80

DON'T "HARD SELL" ANYTHING TO THE GUEST

We shared alternative activities with our guests during their accommodation and some of their plans are made way before their arrival. Programs don't always work out as scheduled. They can compare their plans with your recommendations from time to time. You must tell how they can use their time well in addition to their plans and how many places they can visit with easy transportation. Ensuring trust is very important at this step. They might ask about alternative programs. Don't manipulate them to profit. Don't force them to sell things like city tours, private transfers, shopping tours, or private boat tours. Don't run after them with leaflets in your hands and don't try to make sells by force. The slightest discomfort will come back to you in a harmful way.

81

WAKE UP CALL

Wake-up call means wake-up service. If the next day is the check-out day of our guests, they will sleep with one eye open that night. It's a must for us to let them sleep peacefully. For this reason, the switchboard operator calls the rooms of the guests who will check out the next day. When we call these rooms we ask: "Mr. Brown, Good evening. I'm Laila, your check-out day is tomorrow and your check-out time is 11:00 AM. Would you like to use our wake-up service?" If the answer is positive, we ask, "Would you like a secondary wake-up?" By doing this, we not only give quality service but also remind the check-out time. You also clarify the possibility of extending their stay. Also, the next day, you will be relieved during the operations. If the guest desires a wake-up call, but they don't pick up the phone, the Guest Service team knocks the door to wake them up. We don't want anyone to miss their planes or meetings.

82

MAKE LITTLE GESTURES AND OFFER LITTLE TREATS

The value of the little gestures you make without making cost calculations might be priceless. Our purpose is to make everyone feel at home. While you're hosting a guest in your own house, you offer little treats. Why shouldn't we do the same thing to our guests who preferred our hotel? For example; fruit plate with three pieces, dried nuts and fruits, different kinds of delights, and a special milkshake or little cakes for the guests with children might not cost much but can go a long way. Offering treats takes you one step ahead from courtesy and quality. These little treats can have great comebacks.

83

BE RESOURCEFUL TO THE FAMILIES WITH CHILDREN

In the previous rule, we stated that little treats to our little guests could improve our quality and courtesy. In this situation, the children will be the focus entirely. You can guess how sensitive your guests concerning their children. We must offer options according to the age of our little guests. A baby bed and toys for 0-2 age group, a baby stroller to use in the city; cartoons, DVD films, a play station, and even a babysitter service. The essential matter is having a list of pediatric emergency services working 7/24 at your disposal. You can never know what might happen.

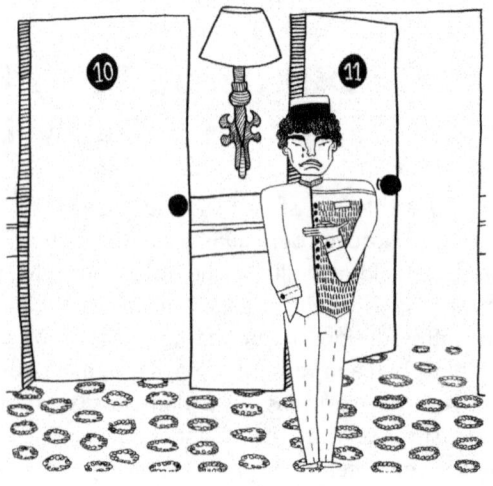

84

RESPECT COMES

BEFORE THE TIP

Who doesn't want to add an extra income to their salary? How can we question an earning as long as it's well deserved? Any service that you give without expecting something will come back at you as much more. Of course, this situation might be exaggerated from time to time. How? The Guest Service has moved the luggage of the guest to their room, and the presentation of the room goes on and on until they get a tip; this is too much. We disrespect our guests by doing that. Also, never react to the amount of the tip your guests give. What you need to do is thank them for preferring our hotel.

85

BE READY FOR EMERGENCIES

We can't know when or where our guests might need us, but emergency numbers should be available at the bulletin boards of each department at your hotel. At the 83rd rule, I would like to give an example of a matter nobody is prepared for but should be; this is my personal experience.

The little three-year-old girl of our guests suddenly became ill. Put yourself in that family's shoes. Guest may run towards you in the lobby in panic, ask for a phone number of pediatric emergency service. Not every hospital has this pediatric emergency department, and your correct guidance might save a life in this situation. You must be ready for everything; you must master the environment of the hotel in case there would be an emergency. In addition to that, keep the numbers of institutions like fire and rescue service, ambulance, police where you can access.

86

KEEP IT CLEAN

Cleaning means removal of dirt and impurities on surfaces, and providing hygiene. In hotels, housekeeping departments do the cleaning, and this department is responsible for almost 80% of the hotel. There is an incredible amount of details to prepare a room after check-out. The path to bringing guest satisfaction to the highest level goes from cleaning. A maid cleans 15 to 17 rooms on average by the industry standards. This department is the department with the highest number of employees in the hotel. You can understand the difficulty of this job. You can never compromise cleaning in the guest satisfaction.

87

PAY ATTENTION TO DND ROOMS!

DND stands for "Do Not Disturb." When the guests don't want to be disturbed, they hang DND signs on the door knob, and they leave the red light on meaning do not disturb. In this case, we don't ask about cleaning and put it into daily floor report. But if this situation still goes on after the second day, we inform the manager on duty, and we call the room. If we can't reach the guest, we check the room with a witness and put the information on the official report. If it is not an emergency such as fire, earthquake, police and law enforcement force, natural disasters; this rule should not be violated by the hotel staff; this is a delicate matter and a common mistake made by the hotel staff.

88

SET THE ROOM TEMPERATURE WISELY

When you see this rule, you might think about how it is related to guest satisfaction. It is. We face this situation usually in the winter with cold weather or in the hot summers. Especially in the intense winter period, if we don't have to change the assignments of the rooms before our guests' check-in to the hotel, the room temperature should always be around 23 Celcius degrees/74 Fahrenheit. If it's the summer period, room temperature should be 20 degrees/68 Fahrenheit. In the periods like this, no guest would want to enter an ice-cold room on a winter day or a boiling room on a summer day. We must pay attention to this matter during the accommodation of our guests. Especially the Front Office should be sensitive while assigning the rooms to the families with kids. It's our greatest wish that our little guests don't get affected by this situation.

89

DON'T SPEAK LOUDLY

The floor hallways of our hotel are the passages to the resting areas of our guests. In addition to the 87th rule where we examined the DND matter, the floor hallways are also a subject of the most received complaints. One of the most significant mistakes is using the vacuum cleaner before our guests wake up. Also, speaking loudly, not closing the doors slowly, walking with heels and making noise will cause guest dissatisfaction. What we need to do first is cleaning the rooms that already checked-out. If there isn't and the guests are still in the room, we need to organize the warehouse and dust the hallways. Remember, we're there to comfort our guests, not to lose their sleep.

90

KEEP THE STAFF TROLLEYS AND HALLWAYS IN AN ORDER

When it comes to organization, we should be an expert. I want to remind you: "Cleanliness is next to godliness." We need to make our guests feel that we are neat and organized. The order also makes it easier for us to finish our work. This situation isn't only the case for the Housekeeping but also for the other departments. But disorder and mess in our hallways cause negativity in the eyes of our guests. Disorder of the floor trolley, the vacuum cleaner, the dirty laundry trolley or the basket of chemicals in the hallways deface the picture of our hotel and causes the floor housekeeper to leave the room while tidying, thus causing a waste of time. I have witnessed the guests having a hard time passing with their luggage because of this mess in a lot of hotels; this isn't a pleasant situation at all.

Orkun Avkan

91

KEEP READY A COMPLETE SET OF HOTEL GUEST AMENITIES

When we say hotel guest amenities, we are talking about the stuff in the room offered to the guests for their personal use. These might include soap, shampoo, body lotion, hair conditioner, cotton buds, little rasp, hair restraint, toilet paper, shoe shine, shoehorn, and lots of other things that we can add. In the hotel industry, where the details designate the quality, the selection of these products is crucial. They must always be complete and ready. If we don't provide these small things carefully, we can trigger more significant problems. We have to find fast solutions for our guests. Some of the hotel guest amenities should be ready at the Front Office department. They should be brought to the room by the Guest Service in the urgent needs of our guests.

92

HAVE A PILLOW MENU

One of the essential privileges we can offer to our guests who preferred us is the pillow menu. Even in the most luxurious hotel, who don't want to use their own pillow? The only way to solve this problem is by providing a rich pillow menu. If we were to make a list of the first things come to mind, we would probably list; silicone pillow, goose down pillow, orthopedic pillow, anti-allergic pillow, slim pillow and child pillow; and the list would go on. Many times I have witnessed guests who carry their pillow in their luggage during their trip. We might spare them from traveling with their pillow if they can pick the closest pillow to their need.

93

PROVIDE TURNDOWN SERVICE

In the hospitality industry, turndown service is the second service given by the housekeeping department after 18.00. The purpose of this service is to prepare the guest's room to sleep. What this means is the services such as making the beds for use, bringing the curtain down, turning down the lights, the treats like candies and delights put on the table, taking the garbage, preparing the bathrobe and slippers beside the bed. These 3-4 minutes of service provides guest satisfaction and quality service.

94

OFFER A GENEROUS ALL-YOU-CAN-EAT BUFFET

The most important meal in our nutrition is breakfast! Even if every hotel can't offer very luxurious amenities, they must at least offer a good breakfast. There are four key elements which make an excellent all-you-can-eat buffet: The freshness of the products in the eyes of a guest that just woke up, the presentation of the plates, the variety of the products and the budget planning. The variety is essential in terms of appealing to everyone. The selection of the products according to the season and freshness strengthen your buffet. Remember, you must first feast our guests' eyes upon. Otherwise, you can get a lot of complaints.

95

OFFER A RIGHT-PRICED AND ABUNDANT MENU

At the beginning of our book, in the 4th rule, we explained the wide range of customer in the hotel industry. We need to prepare a menu that will address a wide range of customers. The menu is the list where our guests can choose their preferences on the paper. The menu reflects your quality and professionalism. The primary objective here is to design and present the menu in a way that your guests can easily understand. You can prove the quality of your menu with the products coming from all over the world. In addition to our updated menu, its price equilibrium is also essential. In this case, the menu that you present must be updated, right priced but also rich with a variety of options.

96

DO IT RIGHT: MINI BAR CHECKS

The little refrigerator put at the disposal of the accommodating guests, which provides extra income for the hotel is called a mini bar. The mini bar contains non-alcoholic or alcoholic drinks, chocolates and little snacks like these. The mini bar checks, organizations, and cleanings are made by the mini bar staff to let the guests use it with pleasure. During the checks, the mini bar staff should pay the utmost attention and shouldn't make mistakes while posting. These posting mistakes sometimes cause our guests to have a difficult time during their check-out. This situation isn't welcomed at the reception. If the guest has canceled a wrong posting, they fill and sign a folio with the canceled product. Even if this process satisfies the guest afterward, it causes losing time during the check-out.

97

GUEST RELATIONS DEPARTMENT

The guest relations department provides communication between the guests and the hotel. They play a big part in solving the guest problems, listening to the recommendations, and applying the requests. The key to repeat customers once again lies here. The guest relations department is responsible for understanding, solving, and taking care of problems or complaints. This department plays a joker role at the hotel.

For this reason, the people who work in the guest relations department should have teamwork capacities with which they can support every department. Their primary duties are meeting the requests and wills of our guests even if they haven't arrived yet, taking an active role in each department at the hotel and excelling the service quality. But also remember that each staff is also a guest relations staff.

98

PAY ATTENTION TO THE ALLERGIES

What we call as allergy is our body reacting in a more sensitive way to some substances. In addition to that, it also includes the reactions of our body to weather changes or some other conditions. Our body has allergies for certain types of food and beverage, medications, dust, smells, and even pollens flying in the air. You can't know the allergies of our guests who come from different corners of the world. You must be ready for a situation like this. Especially the allergy for foods and beverages becomes a big problem for us. As a precaution, each staff in the food & beverage department must have the necessary information concerning the ingredients and always ask the guests if they have allergies before taking their order. Also, the ingredients known as allergic should be mentioned in the labels at the restaurants.

99

TAKE CARE OF YOUR PERSONAL APPEARANCE

Respecting your uniform shows the quality of the hotel. Because of that, personal appearance is an important matter. Missing a button of your uniform, having a food stain and even having little rips bring lots of questions to the mind. The department managers are also responsible for this; they should do necessary checks. You must keep up with the appearance standards. Also, the most critical thing complimentary to your uniform is the name tag. The name tag is indispensable. Take care of your appearance because you're representing your hotel.

100

PROVIDE EASY ACCESS TO INTERNET

The internet is one of the essential needs. The internet, in addition to its easy, fast, cheap, and safe usage, has an impact on personal, social life and business. Depriving our guests of necessity like this, which has a considerable effect on their life can cause a lot of complaints and might even go as far as the guests leaving our hotel. We must keep a continuous and robust service since it's so influential in our daily life. We should provide uninterrupted and fast internet service to our guests.

101

MAKE YOUR HOTEL SAFE AND SECURE

The safety is the primary objective for each staff member. We should pay attention to the safety of our guests and our staff. Providing a peaceful and safe environment is the most critical responsibility of the staff. First and foremost, for natural disasters like fire and earthquake, there should be drills. All the training programs related to safety should be given to the staff and inspected; this is the hotel's responsibility. The employees should take all the training programs concerning safety, read the instructions, and apply them. Every experienced risk should be reported and bird-dogged. Using these safety instructions isn't only valuable in our workplace but also at our home and daily life.

Great Hotel Service

www.ingramcontent.com/pod-product-compliance
Lightning Source LLC
Chambersburg PA
CBHW072135170526
45158CB00004BA/1378